Discover Crabs

by Amanda Trane

© 2017 by Amanda Trane
ISBN: 978-1-53240-2579
eISBN: 978-1-53240-2586
Images licensed from Fotolia.com
All rights reserved.
No portion of this book may be reproduced without express permission of the publisher.
First Edition
Published in the United States by
Xist Publishing
www.xistpublishing.com
PO Box 61593 Irvine, CA 92602

There are many different crabs. All crabs have ten legs. Two of the legs are called claws. This crab has big claws.

This is a crab claw. Crabs use their claws to fight, eat, and talk to other crabs.

All crabs have a hard outer shell. It is called an exoskeleton.

We can see this crab's back, legs and belly.

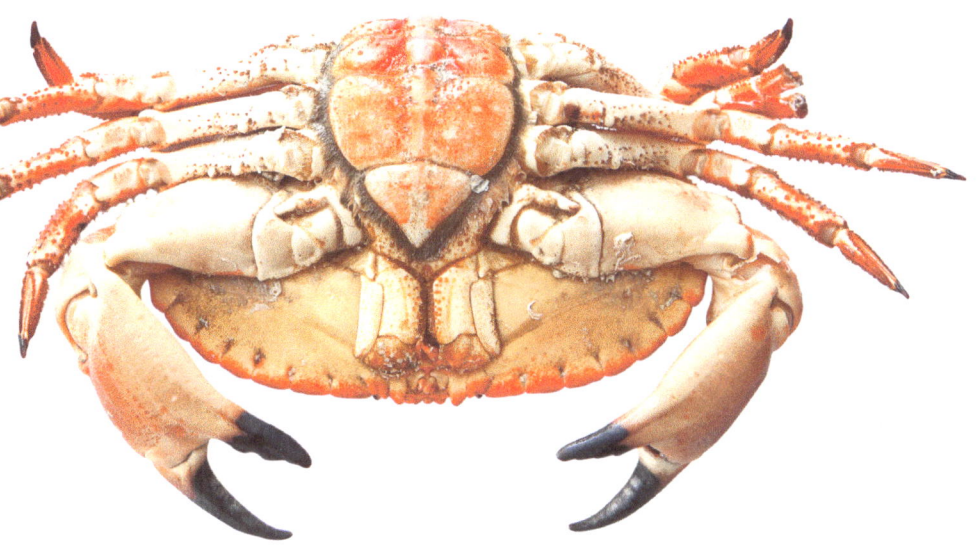

The exoskeleton on the back helps keep the crab safe.

Crab exoskeletons come in many colors. This is an Atlantic Blue Crab.

This patriot crab has red legs, white claws and a blue black.

This moon crab is all red with some orange and purple.

This hermit crab has chosen a white and brown shell.

In the wild, hermit crabs choose from shells from dead sea snails. This hermit crab chose a brown shell.

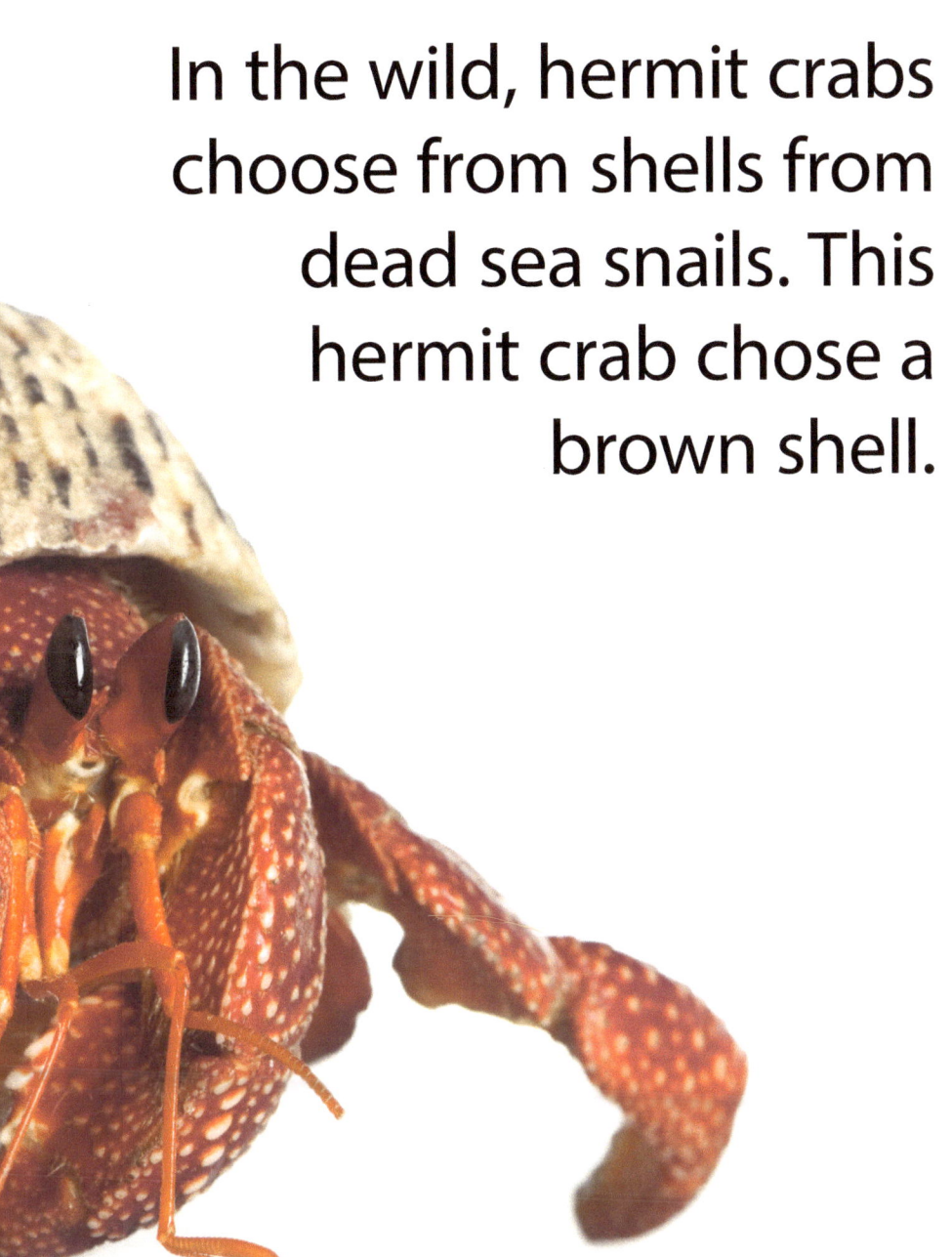

Crabs can be different sizes. Hermit crabs are the perfect size to be a pet.

The king crab can grow to be 6 feet wide.

King crabs live in deep cold water.

Dungeness crabs live in cold bays.

Stone crabs live in shallow warm water.

29

Not all crabs live in the ocean. The red land crab lives in the sand near the ocean.

Some people like to catch and eat crabs. This is a basket of blue crabs.

www.ingramcontent.com/pod-product-compliance
Lightning Source LLC
LaVergne TN
LVHW010020070426
835507LV00001B/21